Animal Ears

by Mary Holland

Most animals have ears. They can be big or small, pointed or round. Part of the ear is always inside the body. Some animals have part of their ear on the outside of their head, where it can be seen by others.

Other animals, like snakes, have ears completely inside their heads. Snakes can hear sound, but they get most of their information from feeling vibrations on the ground with their jaw or their belly.

Ears come in all kinds of shapes. Frogs have ears that are covered with big, round ear drums.

Can you find this green frog's ear drum?

It keeps dirt and water out of the frog's ear and also collects sound. Frogs use their ears to hear the calls of other frogs. Their lungs help them hear some nearby sounds as well!

Not every animal's ears are on their head. Do you know where a katydid's ears are?

On its legs!

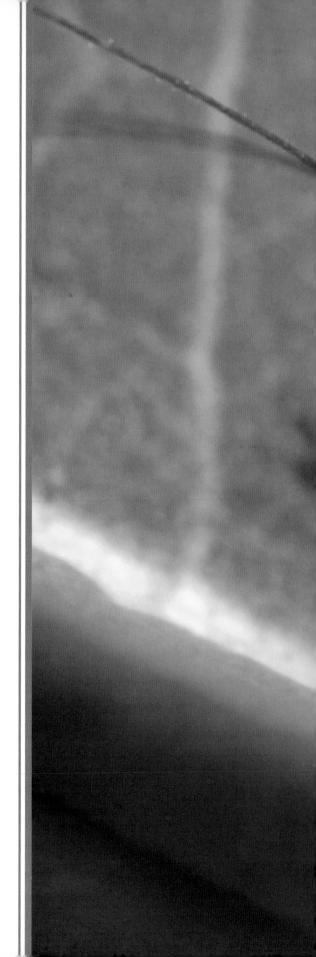

Most animals have two ears. An insect called a praying mantis has only one ear.

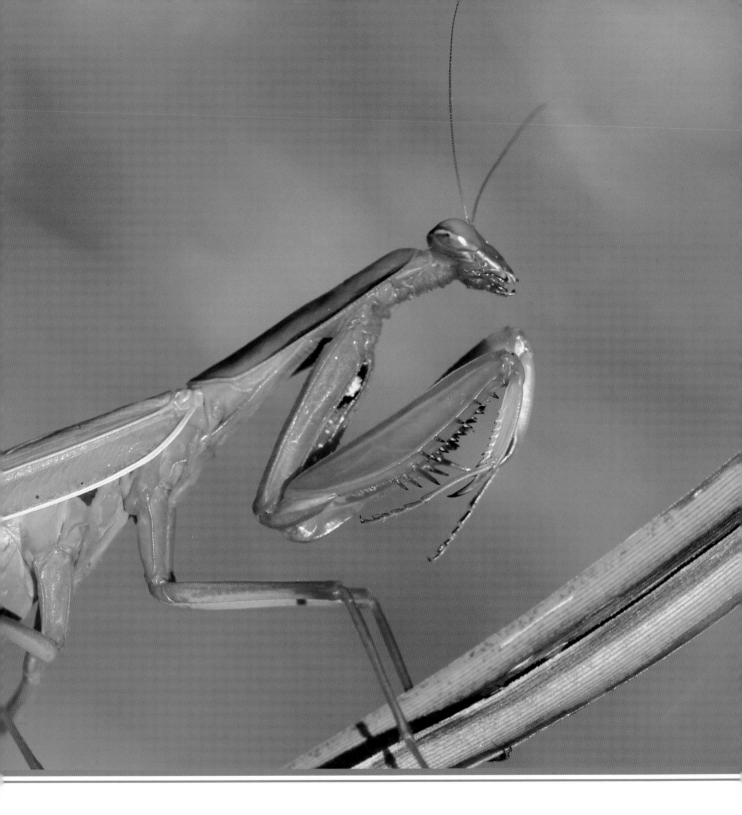

It is located in a groove on the underside of its body, between the two front legs.

Birds have ears, but their ears are hard to see. Their ear holes are on the sides of their head and are often covered with soft feathers.

Owls hear well. They are predators (animals that eat other animals) and hunt at night when it is dark (nocturnal). Why do you think they need to hear well?

Songbirds use their ears in many ways. They are always listening for predators that might be hunting them. Songbirds also use their ears to hear other birds. In the spring, female birds listen to male birds sing to them. Both male and female birds listen for warnings given by other birds.

Woodpeckers eat insects such as beetles, ants, flies, and caterpillars. Many of these insects live in trees.

How do you think woodpeckers know which trees are full of insects? Can they see them?

No, they hear them! Woodpeckers' ears are so sharp that they can hear the rustling and chewing sounds that insects make as they crawl around inside trees.

Like owls, bats are active at night. They can see in the dark, but their eyes are quite small. Bats use their ears more than their eyes to find insects.

Some bats use a sense called echolocation to find insects. They make high-pitched calls. These calls are so high, you and I can't hear them, but bats can. When a bat's calls reach an insect, they bounce off the insect and back to the bat. These echoes tells the bat exactly where the insect is.

Rabbits have big ears to catch sounds well. They can move one ear in one direction and the other ear in another direction in order to hear sounds all around them.

Can you do that?

Rabbits need to be able to hear well so that they can run away from predators, including bobcats, coyotes and hawks. It is hard to sneak up on a rabbit and not be heard.

Bobcats are predators and need to be able to find food (prey). Like rabbits, they can also move one ear at a time. All cats can do this, even house cats.

Predators have to hear well in order to find food. Foxes can hear, see and smell well. They use their ears to hear prey.

Did you know that a red fox can hear a mole digging underground, or a mouse moving through a tunnel under three feet of snow?

Foxes use their ears to communicate. When a fox's ears point forward, other foxes know the fox is curious and listening. Their ears lay flat against their head when they are scared.

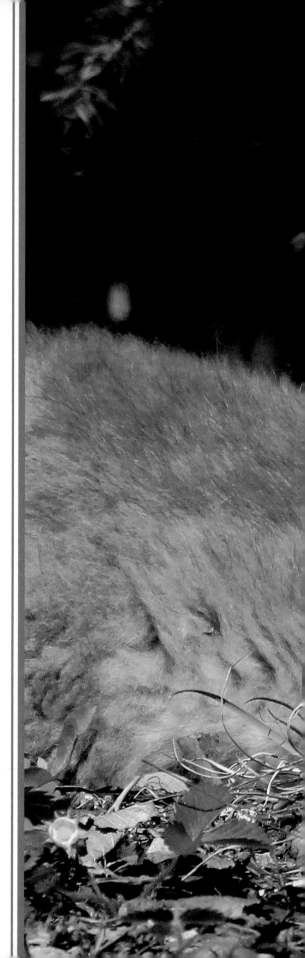

Some ears do more than hear sounds. Beavers have special flaps in their ears that act like ear plugs.

When a beaver dives underwater, the flaps close to keep water from getting into the beaver's ears.

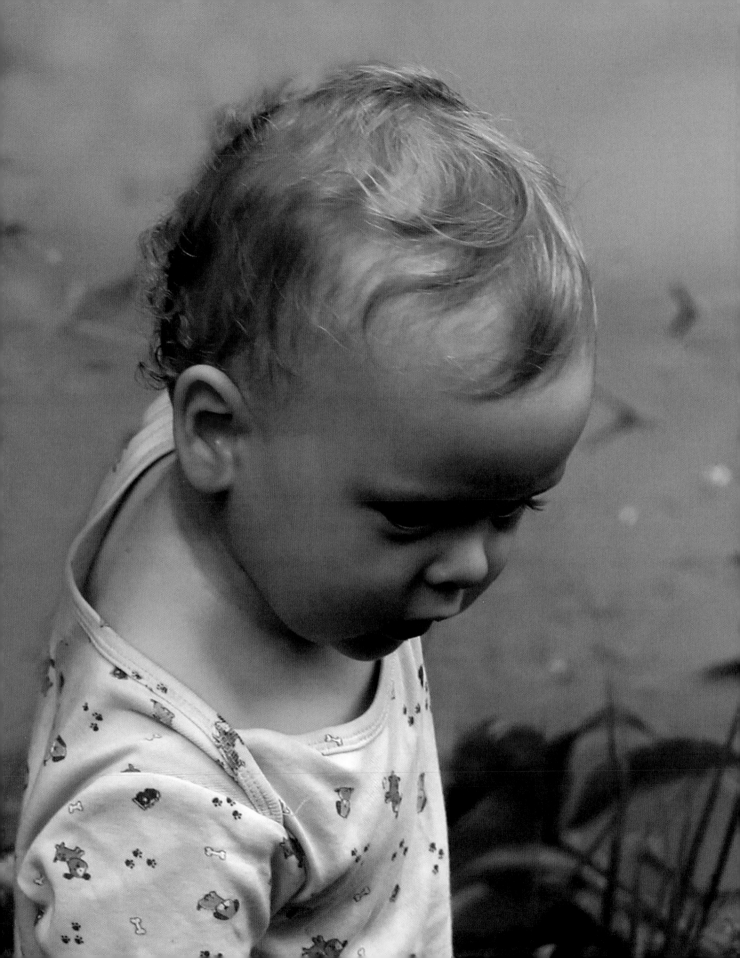

What sounds did
you hear with
your ears today?

For Creative Minds

Animals use their ears to . . .

. . . find a mate.
Some animals, like this moose, use loud mating calls to find companions.

. . . find prey.
By listening carefully, a predator can track the location of their prey.

. . . hear predators.
Keen ears tell prey animals when danger approaches.

. . . communicate with other animals.
Some animals use their ears to show other animals their feelings.

Mix and Match

chipmunk

green frog

Match the animals to their ears. What do you think each animal uses its ears for?

opossum

black bear

1

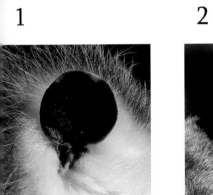

2

3

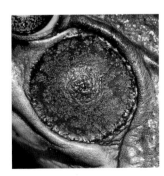

4

Answers: 1) opossum. 2) black bear. 3) green frog. 4) chipmunk.

How Do Ears Hear?

Sound starts with movement. A molecule vibrates—it moves quickly back and forth. It bumps the molecule next to it and sets it vibrating. Molecules of air around them move as each one is bumped by another molecule. The vibration spreads out in waves. They move out away from the starting point like ripples when you drop a pebble in water.

There are tiny hairs inside a person's ear. They are too small to see without a microscope. These hairs vibrate when the sound touches them. The brain understands that vibration as sound.

Ears don't just hear sound, they can also tell where the sound is coming from.

Humans have one ear on each side of their head. When a sound wave travels, it touches the ears at different times. This difference is so small you probably don't think you can notice.

But the brain notices that difference! It uses that time difference to tell where the sound came from. If the sound touched the left ear before it touched the right ear, then the person knows the sound came from the left.

This boy heard a sound and turned toward it. Do you think the sound came from his right or his left?

Did you know?

Millions of people in the United States are **deaf** or **hard of hearing**. They cannot hear sound, or can only hear some sound.

Many people lose their hearing as they get older.

Can you hear? Do you know anybody who cannot hear, or who cannot hear well? Do you know any older people who cannot hear as well as they used to?

Ear Questions

Why do some animals have very small ears?

hairy-tailed mole

Moles, voles and shrews have small ears compared to the size of their bodies. These animals live underground and have to travel quickly and easily through tiny tunnels. If you lived in a small tunnel under the ground and had large flaps on your ears, what would happen to them as you ran through the tunnel?

How do owls hear so well?

great grey owl

Many owls have feathers that form circles around their eyes (facial discs). The feathers in the disc direct sounds to the birds' ears.

Some owls have one ear that is higher on their head than the other ear. This helps them tell what direction a sound is coming from.

Can ears do anything but hear?

red fox

Yes. Some animals, such as rabbits and hares, use their ears to cool their bodies. Heat escapes from their ears. Ears help animals, including humans, keep their balance. Many animals use their ears to communicate their mood.

Thanks to Tabbi Kinion, Statewide Education Coordinator for Colorado Parks and Wildlife, and Sarah Chatwood at the Montana Audubon Center for verifying the accuracy of the information in this book.

Library of Congress Cataloging-in-Publication Data

Names: Holland, Mary, 1946- , author.
Title: Animal ears / by Mary Holland.
Description: Mount Pleasant, SC : Arbordale Publishing, 2018. | Audience: Ages 4 to 8. | Audience: Grades K to 3.
Identifiers: LCCN 2017042959 (print) | LCCN 2017048651 (ebook) | ISBN 9781607184805 (English Downloadable eBook) | ISBN 9781607184904 (English Interactive Dual-Language eBook) | ISBN 9781607184850 (Spanish Downloadable eBook) | ISBN 9781607185161 (Spanish Interactive Dual-Language eBook) | ISBN 9781607184478 (English hardcover) | ISBN 9781607184522 (English pbk.) | ISBN 9781607184638 (Spanish pbk.)
Subjects: LCSH: Ear--Juvenile literature.
Classification: LCC QL948 (ebook) | LCC QL948 .H65 2018 (print) | DDC 612.8/5--dc23
LC record available at https://lccn.loc.gov/2017042959

Translated into Spanish: *Orejas de los animales*

Lexile® Level: 560L

Keywords: physical adaptations, ears, hearing, senses, sound (FCM)

Animals in this book include: coyote (cover), black bear (title page), red-bellied snake, green frog, katydid, praying mantis, barred owl, male rose-breasted grosbeak, yellow-bellied sapsucker, big brown bat, eastern cottontail, bobcat, red fox, beaver, human (author's grandson, Otis Brown).

Bibliography:
Hickman, Pamela M. *Animal senses.* Toronto, Kids Can, 2015.
Holland, Mary. *Naturally Curious: A Photographic Field Guide and Month-By-Month Journey Through the Fields, Woods, and Marshes of New England.* North Pomfret, VT: Trafalgar Square Books, 2010.

To Otis, who is such a good listener!—MH

Manufactured in China, December 2017
This product conforms to CPSIA 2008
First Printing

Arbordale Publishing
Mt. Pleasant, SC 29464
www.ArbordalePublishing.com

Text Copyright 2018 © by Mary Holland